Doug Fields lives in So. CA where he writes books and
speaks about marriage and parenting.
DOUGFIELDS.COM

Jason is a husband, father of 5 (including triples) and an artist
who loves to make stuff everyday.
PEARPOD.COM

Soul Hydration Books
29883 Santa Margarita Parkway,
Rancho Santa Margarita, CA 92692
Info@SoulHydrationBooks.com
SoulHydrationBooks.com

52 THINGS I WANT YOU TO KNOW...

this book is for...

5 things that make me proud.

1.

2.

3.

4.

5.

i might not always say it. these are only the top 5.
i will tell you more in person.

5 movies

that i want you to see sometime + here's why

my 3 heroes! and here's why

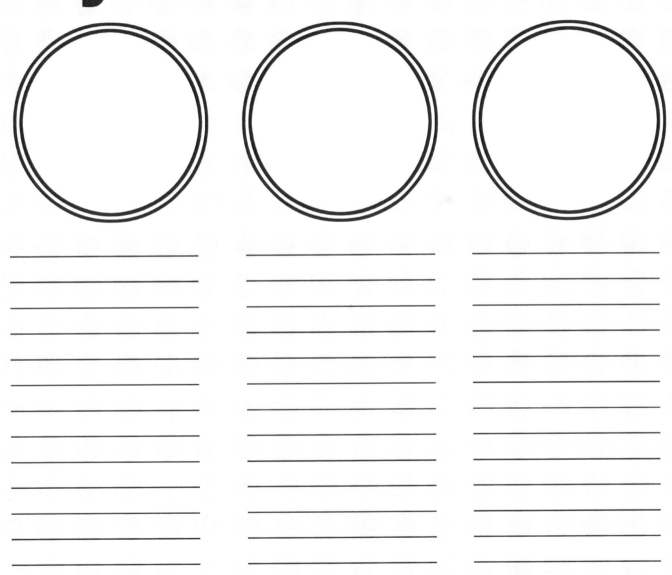

now figure out who your 3 heroes are!

ok, this is one of those really big questions!

what "happens" after we die?

_____
_____
_____
_____
_____
_____
_____
_____
_____
_____
_____
_____
_____
_____
_____
_____
_____
_____
_____
_____
_____
_____
_____
_____
_____
_____

When you fail, flop, fizzle, flounder or screw-up, here's what i want you to know...

and here's a time when i bungled & blundered it...

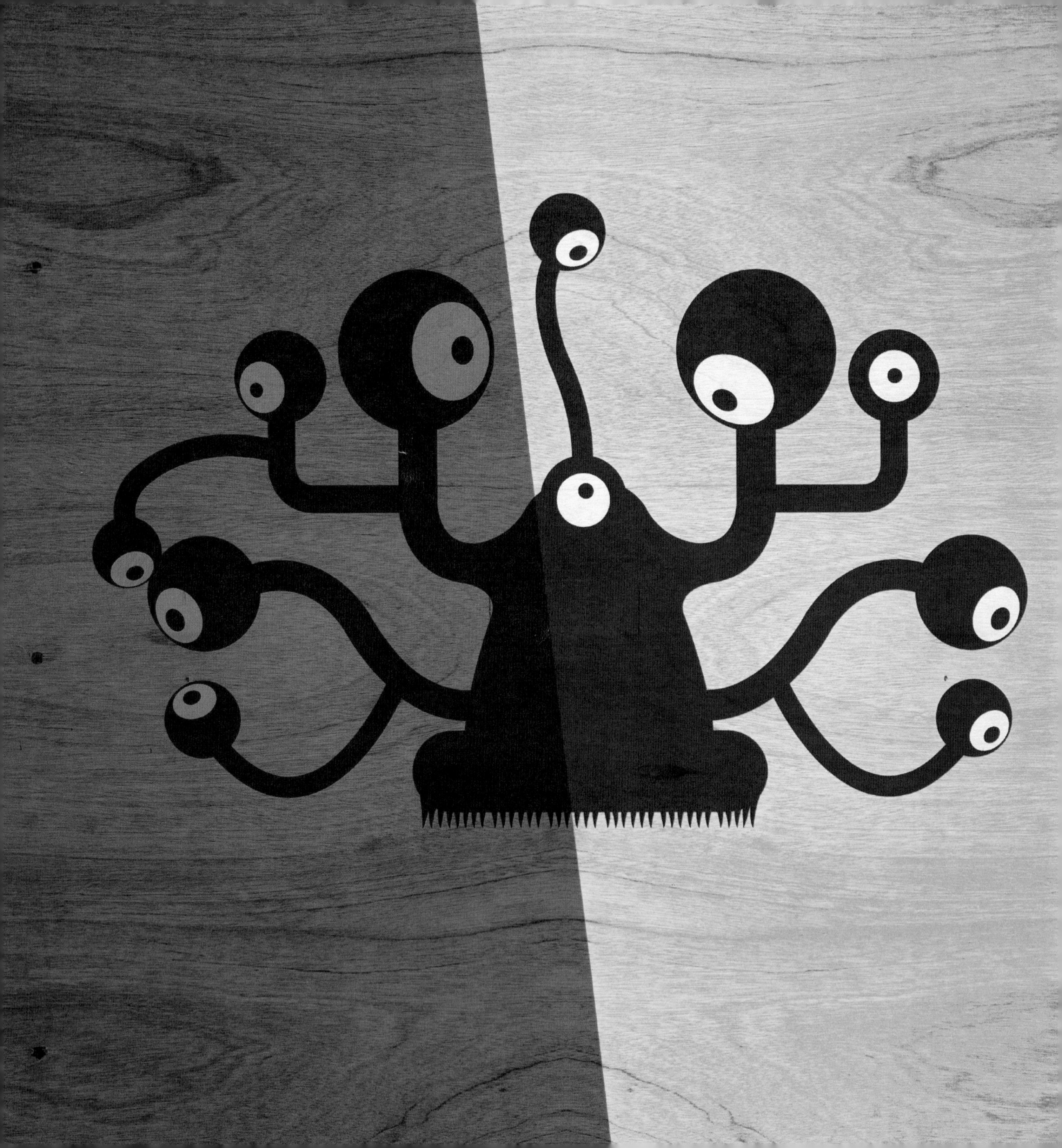

here are 3 risks i wish i would have taken
and why i was too afraid.

when you were born
my life changed
in these 3 ways

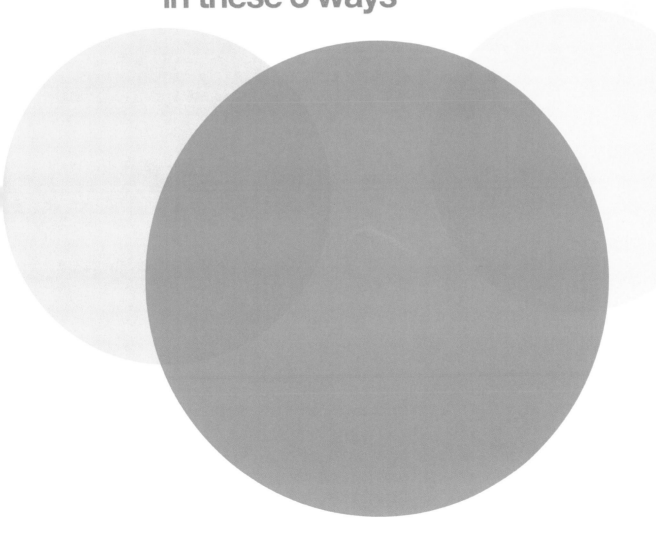

i could probably have
guided you
better if i

5 heroic things
that I love about

_____ (mom/dad/grandma/grandpa)

you are unique

and unlike anyone else in the world because

pssst! here's what i believe about being physically intimate with someone else.

(and why i believe that)

here are 3 ways

you can know i love you.

ere are 3 things I hope you'll learn/steal/inherit from me.

nd here's 1 way how i hope you'll be different from me.

vote your conscience.
here are my top issues for
how and why i vote for someone.

you make me

smile

when you

contrary to what you might think, i don't have all the answers.

(here are some things that totally confuse me)

what???

here are a few of my best ideas on how to really love your neighbor!

my favorite books that i hope you will read someday.

(or listen to the audio book, or at least see the movie)

_____   _____

_____   _____

_____   _____

_____   _____

_____   _____

_____   _____

_____   _____

_____   _____

_____   _____

sometimes i get scared of

another really big question is

why is there so much evil in the world? and how you can deal with it.

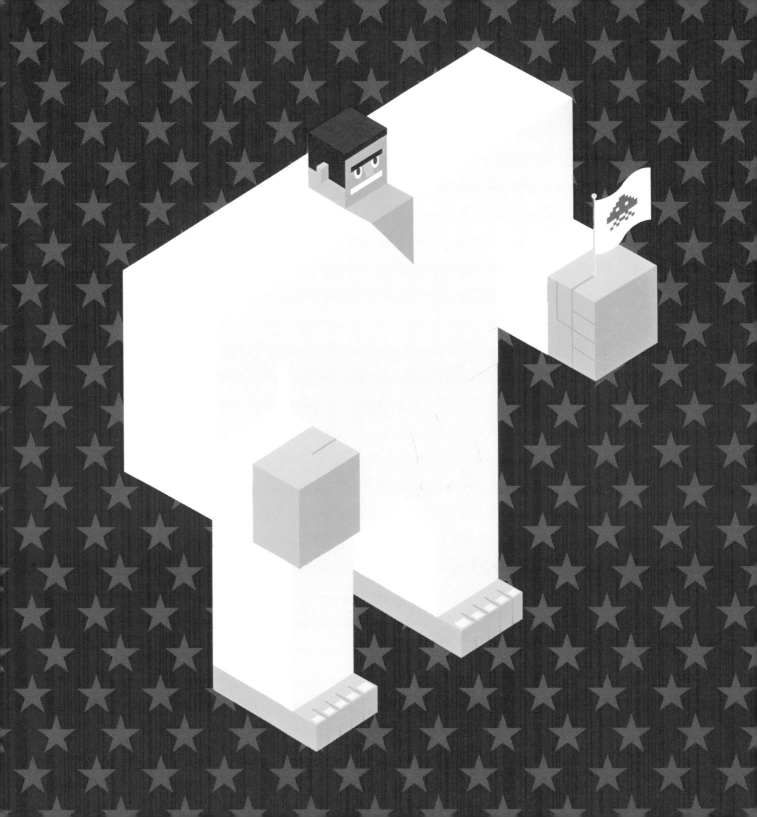

here's how i feel about military service, war, veterans, and patriotism.

_____

_____

_____

_____

_____

_____

_____

_____

_____

_____

_____

_____

you don't need to follow the crowd. here's why

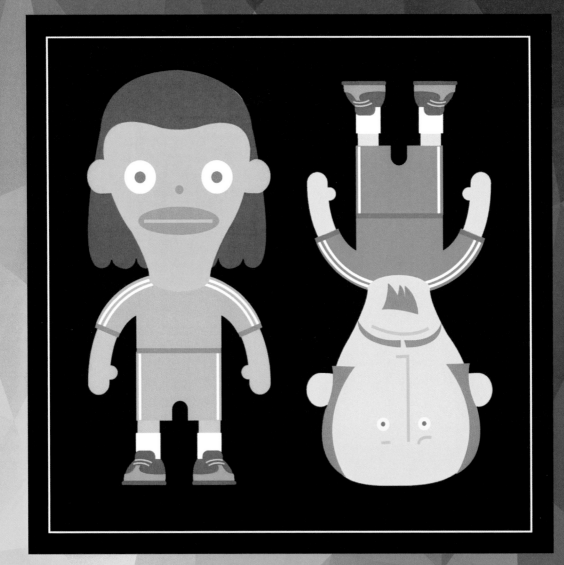

a couple things i want to share with you about my faith journey.

here are two habits i wish i would have developed at a younger age.

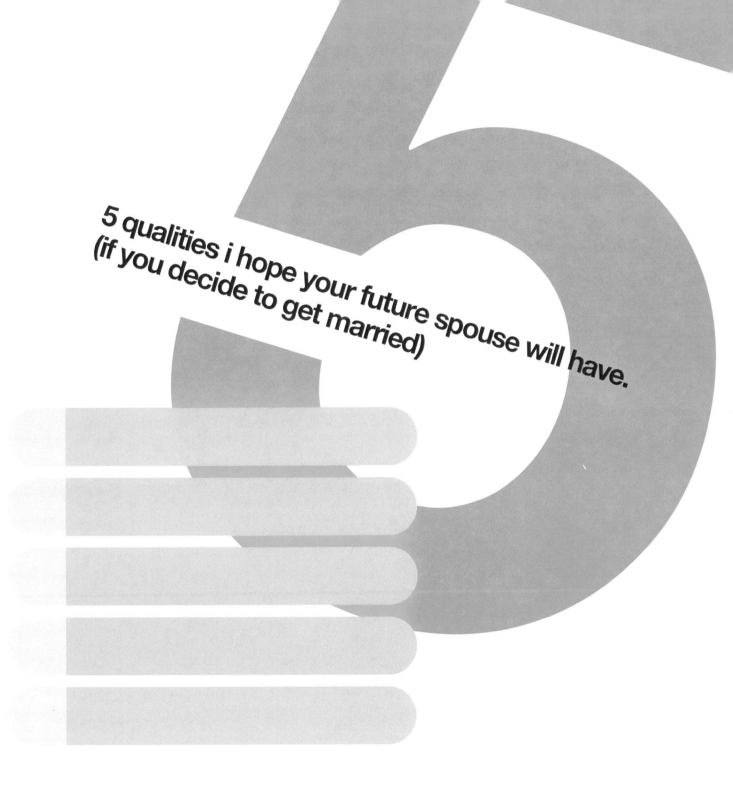

5 qualities i hope your future spouse will have.
(if you decide to get married)

i see you as amazing and talented in these ways.

a few thoughts about cars.

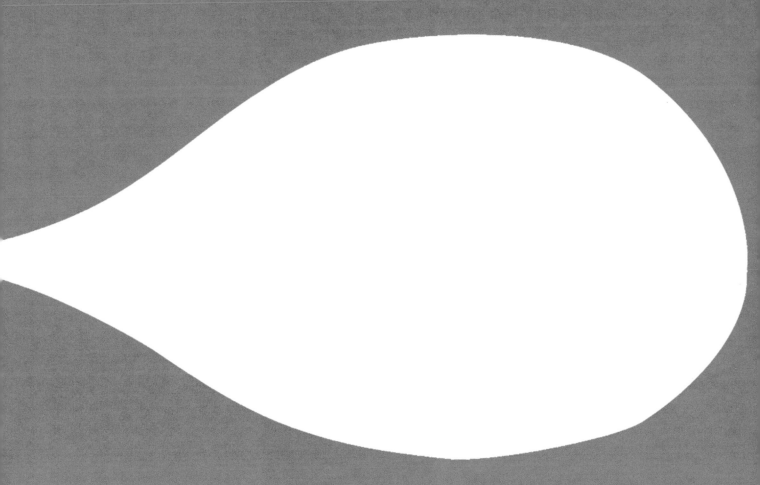

my favorite songs...
go listen to them!

inspiration, love, sadness, suffering, joy, motivation, passion, peace, & soundtracks to life!

_____

_____

_____

_____

here's what i know about God

and what i hope you know too.

people will hurt you and when they do here's what i hope you'll do.

if you become
a parent, you
will be amazing at

some favorite foods i hope you try

sometimes i sing
the blues. here are
a couple social issues
that break my heart.

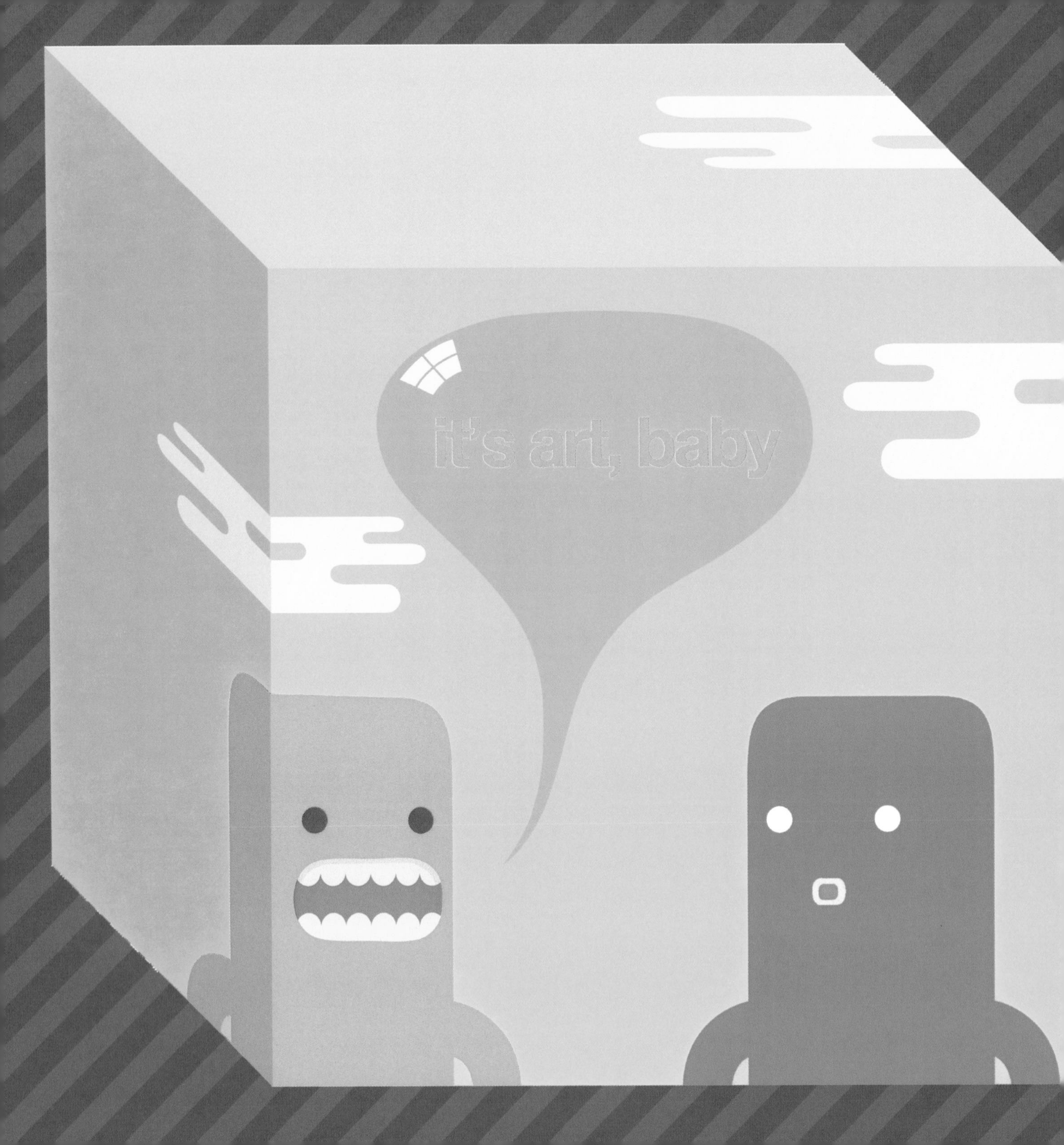
it's art, baby

here are some artists that will make your life better by discovering their work

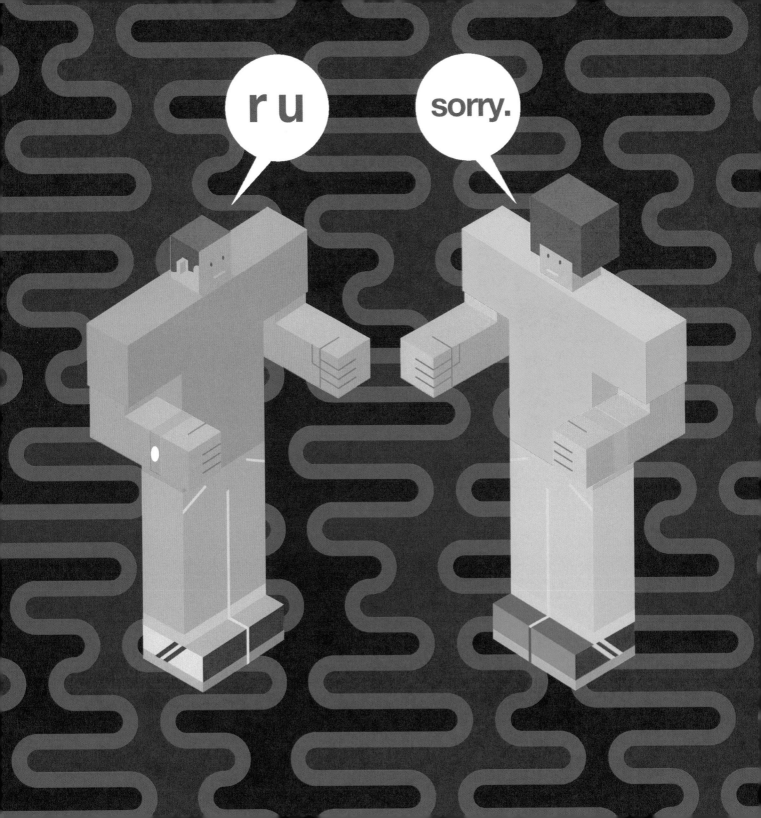

what i've learned about forgiveness

dating.

here's some advice

if i could encourage
you to do do one thing
to make the world
a better place

if i could insert one
character quality into
your life it would be.

here are 3 reasons i fell in love with your _____
mom/dad

when it comes
to money,
i want you to

if you are ever thinking about
ENDING
your own life...
here's what i want
you to know.

favorite phrases my parents used to say.

i don't want
you to be
afraid to talk
to me about.

a favorite photo of you.

(here's why i love it!)

a couple things about
our family heritage.

the internet.*

here is where i think you need to be careful.

when i learned i was going to be a parent.

places i hope you will visit.

when you boil it all down - here's what i think is most

important

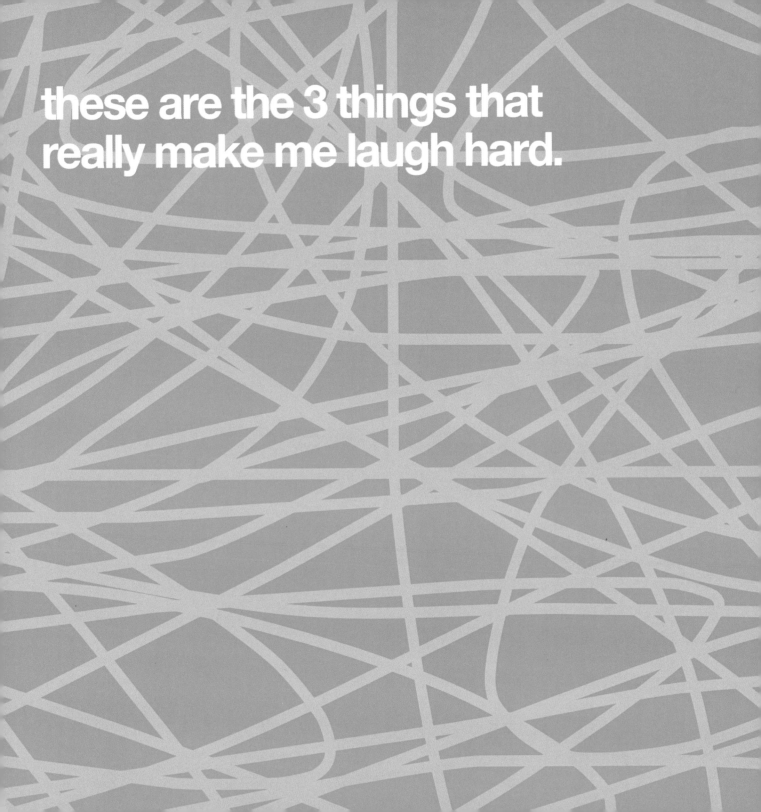

these are the 3 things that really make me laugh hard.

so far, the most embarrassing thing that has ever happened to me was

○ i am a good artist.
○ i am not _a good artist.

Let me show you by drawing a horse:

a little more about me, my favorite

color_____

sport's team_____

tv show (tv, what's that?)_____

musician_____

joke_____

website_____

movie_____

vacation spot_____

type of exercise_____

when i'm real old you'll need to

_____

some medical conditions you'll need to be aware of

_____

Made in the USA
Las Vegas, NV
15 January 2022

41435665R00069